On the Shortness of Life

A Stoic Guide to Time, Meaning, and Living Fully

A Modern Translation

Adapted for the Contemporary Reader

Seneca

Translated by Tim Zengerink

© Copyright 2025. All rights reserved.

It is not legal to reproduce, duplicate, or transmit any part of this document in either electronic means or in printed format. Recording of this publication is strictly prohibited and any storage of this document is not allowed unless with written permission from the publisher except for the use of brief quotations in a book review.

PREFACE
MESSAGE TO THE READER

Dear Reader,

Thank you for choosing this edition; it is more than just a book—you are reading a living thread of humanity's literary heritage.

We'd like to invite you to **gain immediate, unlimited digital & audiobook access** to hundreds of the most treasured literary classics ever written—along with the option to **secure deluxe paperback, hardcover & box set editions at printing cost**. Together, we can **spark a new global literary renaissance** alongside our small, independent publishing house called "The Library of Alexandria."

Thousands of years ago, the Library of Alexandria stood as a beacon of knowledge—until it was lost to history. We aim to reignite that spirit of preservation and discovery right now, in the modern age—only this time, it's accessible to all, in every language and every format.

Picture a world where every timeless classic, novel, poem, or philosophical treatise is not only available to read but also updated for today's readers—modernized, translated into any language or dialect, and ready to enjoy in any format you choose, whether that is in an eBook, audiobook, paperback, or deluxe hardcover & box set version a printing cost.

By joining our movement to **rebuild the modern Library of Alexandria**, you become part of an unprecedented mission to offer:

- **Unlimited Audiobook & eBook Access to the Greatest Classics of All Time**

    Instantly explore thousands of legendary works, from Plato and Shakespeare to Jane Austen and Leo Tolstoy. All are instantly ready to read or listen to, giving you a complete literary universe at your fingertips.

- **Paperback & Deluxe Editions at Printing Costs:**

    Purchase any title in a paperback, deluxe hardbound, or deluxe boxset edition at printing costs, shipped right to your doorstep. Curate your personal library of Alexandria with editions worthy of display—crafted to last, designed to captivate, and delivered straight to your door.

- **Modern translations for Contemporary Readers in all languages and dialects**

    Discover a vast selection of classics reimagined in clear, current language—no more struggling with outdated phrases or obscure references. Next to the original versions, we aim to offer translations in as many languages and dialects as possible.

As we continue our translation efforts and add new languages, readers everywhere can connect with these works as if they were written today. ***By bridging linguistic divides, you're contributing to ensuring that these timeless stories become more meaningful, accessible, and inspiring for people across the globe.***

- **Your Personal Library of Alexandria:**

  Over the months and years, you'll curate a unique physical archive of classics—each volume a testament to your taste, curiosity, and love of knowledge. It's not just about owning books—it's about curating a cultural legacy you'll cherish and pass down for generations to come.

- **Join a Global Literary Renaissance:**

  Your support fuels an ongoing mission: allowing us to reinvest in offering deluxe print editions (including special boxsets) at their true cost, broaden the range of available formats and translations, and extend the reach of these works to new audiences worldwide. By joining today, you're not just preserving a legacy of masterpieces; ***you set in motion a powerful wave of literary accessibility.***

We are more than a publisher—we're a movement, and we can't do it alone. Your support lets us scale our mission, preserving and reimagining history's greatest works for tomorrow's readers.

Become a Torchbearer of knowledge.

Thank you for picking up this book and allowing us into your literary journey. As you turn the pages, know that you're part of something larger: a global effort to keep these stories alive, share their wisdom across borders and generations, and spark a true cultural revival for the modern era.

If this resonates with you—please consider taking the next step. By visiting:
www.libraryofalexandria.com

With gratitude and a shared love of knowledge,

The Modern Library of Alexandria Team

Visit:

www.libraryofalexandria.com

Or scan the code below:

LETTER 49

ON THE SHORTNESS OF LIFE

A person is indeed truly lazy and careless, my dear Lucilius, if he only remembers a friend when he sees a place that reminds him of that friend. But sometimes, familiar places bring back a feeling of loss that we've kept hidden inside. They don't just bring back dead memories but wake them up from where they've been sleeping, like how seeing a lost friend's favorite slave, cloak, or house can renew the sadness, even if time has made it softer.

Now, look at Campania, especially Naples and your beloved Pompeii. When I saw them, they made me miss you a lot. I can picture you clearly in my mind, like I'm about to say goodbye to you. I see you trying hard to hold back your tears but not being able to stop the emotions that rise up just when you try to control them. It feels like I lost you just a moment ago because, when we use our memory, everything feels like it happened just a short while ago.

It seems like just a moment ago that I was a young boy sitting in the philosopher Sotion's school, just a moment ago that I started working as a lawyer, just a moment ago that I lost the desire to practice law, and just a moment ago that I lost the ability to do it. Time flies incredibly fast, especially when we look back at it. When we're focused on what's happening now, we don't notice how fast time is passing because it moves so gently and quickly.

Do you wonder why? All the time that has passed is in the same place; it all looks the same to us, like it's all mixed together. Everything slips into the same emptiness. Also, something that is so short can't have long periods within it. The time we spend living is just a tiny point, or even smaller than a point. But this tiny bit of time, short as it is, nature has tricked us into thinking it's longer than it really is. She has divided it into parts like infancy, childhood, youth, the gradual slope from youth to old age, and old age itself is yet another part. How many steps there are for such a short climb!

It feels like just a moment ago that I saw you off on your journey, and yet this "moment ago" makes up a good part of our existence. This existence is so brief that we should remember it will soon end altogether. In other years, time didn't seem to go by so quickly; now, it seems to fly by faster than I can believe, maybe because I feel that the end is getting closer, or maybe because I've started to notice and count my losses.

For this reason, I'm even more upset that some people spend most of this short time on things that don't matter—time that, no matter how carefully we protect it, isn't enough even for the important things. Cicero said that even if he had twice as many days to live, he wouldn't have time to read the lyric poets. You could say the same thing about people who study complicated arguments, but they are foolish in a sadder way. The lyric poets admit that they are writing for fun, but these people think they're doing something serious.

I'm not saying you shouldn't look at these complex arguments, but you should only glance at them, like saying a quick hello at the door, just to avoid being tricked into thinking they're really valuable. Why stress yourself out and lose weight over some problem that it's smarter to ignore than to solve? When a soldier is relaxed and traveling at his own pace, he can stop to look at small things along the way, but when the enemy is close behind and the order is given to speed up, he has to throw away everything he picked up during peaceful times.

I don't have time to figure out the tricky details of words or to show off how clever I am with them. Look at the enemy gathering, the gates locked tight, and weapons ready for battle. I need a strong heart to listen to this noise of battle all around me without flinching.

Everyone would rightly think I was crazy if, while the older men and women were piling up rocks for the walls, and the young men in armor inside the gates were waiting or even asking for the order to attack, and the enemy's spears were shaking our gates, and the ground was trembling with mines and tunnels, I sat there doing nothing, asking silly questions like, "What you haven't lost, you still have. But you haven't lost any horns. So, you must have horns," or other nonsense like that.

And yet, you might think I'm just as crazy if I spend my energy on that kind of thing, because even now, I'm under siege. But in the first case, the danger would only be from the outside, with a wall between me and the enemy; but now, the danger of death is right here with me. I don't have time for such foolishness; I have a big task ahead of me. What should I do? Death is close behind me, and life is slipping away.

Teach me something to help me face these troubles. Help me stop trying to run away from death, and help me stop letting life slip through my fingers.

Give me the courage to face hardships; make me calm in the face of what I can't avoid. Help me make the most of the short time I have. Show me that the value of life doesn't depend on how long it is, but on how well I use it. Also, show me that it's possible, or even common, for someone who has lived a long life to have actually lived very little. Tell me when I lie down to sleep, "You might not wake up again!" And when I wake up, "You might not go to sleep again!" Tell me when I leave my house, "You might not come back!" And when I come back, "You might not leave again!"

You're wrong if you think that there's only a thin line between life and death on a sea voyage. No, that line is just as thin everywhere. It's just that we don't always see death so close by, but he's always just as near.

Take away these shadowy fears, and then it will be easier for you to teach me the lessons I'm ready to learn. When we were born, nature made us capable of learning, and she gave us reason, not perfect, but capable of being perfected.

Teach me about justice, duty, self-discipline, and the two types of purity—one that keeps us from harming others and one that keeps us true to ourselves. If you don't lead me down the wrong paths, I'll reach my goal more easily. As the tragic poet says: "The language of truth is simple." So we shouldn't make that language complicated; nothing is less suitable for a person with great goals than tricky cleverness. Farewell.

The End

Thank you for Reading

Dear Reader,

We hope this timeless classic has sparked your imagination and enriched your literary journey. Now that you've turned the final page, we want to share a vision for the future of reading—one where every classic you've ever wanted to explore is at your fingertips, in a format that best suits your life.

We'd like to invite you to **gain immediate, unlimited digital & audiobook access** to hundreds of the most treasured literary classics ever written—along with the option to **secure deluxe paperback, hardcover & box set editions at printing cost**. Together, we can **spark a new global literary renaissance** alongside our small, independent publishing house called "The Library of Alexandria."

Thousands of years ago, the Library of Alexandria stood as a beacon of knowledge—until it was lost to history. We aim to reignite that spirit of preservation and discovery right now, in the modern age—only this time, it's accessible to all, in every language and every format.

Picture a world where every timeless classic, novel, poem, or philosophical treatise is not only available to read but also updated for today's readers—modernized, translated into any language or dialect, and ready to enjoy in any format you choose, whether that is in an eBook, audiobook, paperback, or deluxe hardcover & box set version a printing cost.

By joining our movement to **rebuild the modern Library of Alexandria**, you become part of an unprecedented mission to offer:

- **Unlimited Audiobook & eBook Access to the Greatest Classics of All Time**

  Instantly explore thousands of legendary works, from Plato and Shakespeare to Jane Austen and Leo Tolstoy. All are instantly ready to read or listen to, giving you a complete literary universe at your fingertips.

- **Paperback & Deluxe Editions at Printing Costs:**

  Purchase any title in a paperback, deluxe hardbound, or deluxe boxset edition at printing costs, shipped right to your doorstep. Curate your personal library of Alexandria with editions worthy of display—crafted to last, designed to captivate, and delivered straight to your door.

- **Modern translations for Contemporary Readers in all languages and dialects**

  Discover a vast selection of classics reimagined in clear, current language—no more struggling with outdated phrases or obscure references. Next to the original versions, we aim to offer translations in as many languages and dialects as possible.

  As we continue our translation efforts and add new languages, readers everywhere can connect with these works as if they were written today. *By bridging linguistic divides, you're contributing to ensuring that these timeless stories become more meaningful, accessible, and inspiring for people across the globe.*

- **Your Personal Library of Alexandria:**

  Over the months and years, you'll curate a unique physical archive of classics—each volume a testament to your taste, curiosity, and love of knowledge. It's not just about owning books—it's about curating a cultural legacy you'll cherish and pass down for generations to come.

- **Join a Global Literary Renaissance:**

  Your support fuels an ongoing mission: allowing us to reinvest in offering deluxe print editions (including special boxsets) at their true cost, broaden the range of available formats and translations, and extend the reach of these works to new audiences worldwide.

By joining today, you're not just preserving a legacy of masterpieces; *you set in motion a powerful wave of literary accessibility.*

We are more than a publisher—we're a movement, and we can't do it alone. Your support lets us scale our mission, preserving and reimagining history's greatest works for tomorrow's readers.

Become a Torchbearer of knowledge.

Thank you for picking up this book and allowing us into your literary journey. As you turn the pages, know that you're part of something larger: a global effort to keep these stories alive, share their wisdom across borders and generations, and spark a true cultural revival for the modern era.

If this resonates with you—please consider taking the next step. By visiting:
www.libraryofalexandria.com

With gratitude and a shared love of knowledge,

The Modern Library of Alexandria Team

Visit:

www.libraryofalexandria.com

Or scan the code below:

www.ingramcontent.com/pod-product-compliance
Lightning Source LLC
LaVergne TN
LVHW030636080426
835512LV00022B/3477